A Pictorial History
— OF —
The Willamette Valley

This book was made possible through the generous support of

Statesman Journal

Copyright© 1997 • ISBN: 1-891395-07-6

Published by Pediment Publishing, a division of The Pediment Group, Inc. Portland, Oregon.

FOREWORD

History is everywhere in this Willamette Valley.

It infuses the Zorn homestead, built near Champoeg in 1867 and still in the Zorn family today. It's at the heart of Dallas' town square, a haven of small-town calm laid out around a courthouse built in 1899. It lives on in the dormers and gables of the neighborhoods ringing Salem's downtown.

History is not something detached and distant. It's a part of the landscape that we see every day. It's a work in progress, a backdrop for our lives.

Accordingly, the *Statesman Journal* is pleased to present A Pictorial History of the Willamette Valley, a collection of more than 300 images from the past.

To leaf through these pages is to journey into a bygone era. We see the venerable state Capitol that burned in 1935. We see rustic farmhouses, horses and buggies, steam locomotives, the harvest of such forgotten crops as flax. We see festivals that are no more – such as Salem's Cherry Festival – and organizations that have faded away, like the Stayton Cornet Band.

But many of the images here are readily recognizable, even if they were captured years ago. The shapes of downtown Salem's Reed Opera House and Grand Theater and Mount Angel's famous abbey resonate even in black and white.

We're reminded of other links with the past, too. In recent times, we have endured such disasters as flooding on the Willamette River – the same misery that afflicted valley residents in the 1800s and earlier this century.

In the past, as now, life here has been an interwoven fabric of work and play, misfortune and success. All of those realities are illustrated in these pages.

We owe thanks to the Oregon State Library, with its extensive photo collections, and to a local historian, Al Jones, who gave generously of his time and effort.

This book is not intended as a comprehensive history of Salem and the Willamette Valley. Rather, it is a kaleidoscope of images of what was – and often, of what still is.

Sara M. Bentley
President and Publisher
Statesman Journal

A Bird's Eye View

It is from above that the true sweep of change in the valley comes into focus. Views from hilltops, and later from airplanes, show towns like Salem spreading away from their nucleuses, across fields to the north and east, over hills to the west and south.

The beginning point for white settlement in the mid-valley was along lower Mill Creek, where native Americans once gathered. There, in the 1840s, Methodist missionaries built a sawmill – and the first house in Salem.

For decades, Salem's proportions remained modest.

When it was moved here from Portland in the 1860s, the Oregon State Penitentiary was far beyond the city's eastern fringe. At the turn of the century, a view north from what is now Vista Avenue SE was of rolling fields, with Salem huddled in the distance.

Now, stretching a dozen miles from the South Salem hills to the tip of Keizer, the community bears little resemblance to the bird's eye views of old – except in one way.

Even photos from early this century show a grassy expanse downtown, with the Capitol at its center. Today, in spite of all that has changed, that heart of Salem remains.

A view up Trade Street in Salem looking toward the Capitol and Willamette University in 1889. The locomotive in the photo is headed east along Trade Street toward the present 12th Street. The stacked wood was used by the Churchill Sash and Door Manufacturing Co. and the Western Fanning Mill.
Published with permission of The Oregon State Library (B-9-6)

An early view of Salem, looking northeast from a south Salem hill, circa 1910. *Published with permission of The Oregon State Library*

View of Salem from the state Capitol, circa 1894. Willson Park had shaped trees and a quarter-mile bicycle track and Salem City Hall was under construction at the time.

Aerial view of Mount Angel Abbey and college.
Published with permission of The Oregon State Library (WPA-4#339)

Woodburn in 1893. The view is from the water tower showing the railroad depot and other buildings from Front Street west.

Published with permission of The Oregon State Library (13-1)

A view of Salem looking northeast from the Capitol toward the State Hospital, circa 1900. *Photo courtesy Al Jones*

Aerial view of the State Fairgrounds in Salem.

Published with permission of The Oregon State Library (29-6)

Scotts Mills, 1949.

A bird's eye view of Silverton, circa 1920. *Photo courtesy Silverton Country Historical Society*

Silverton from West Main hill looking down Main Street, circa 1908.
Photo courtesy Silverton Country Historical Society

A view of Stayton, circa 1908. *Photo courtesy Santiam Historical Society*

Mill City, circa 1911. *Photo courtesy Santiam Historical Society*

This view of Salem is looking west from the Capitol, circa 1900. The Marion County Courthouse is to the left center.

Published with permission of The Oregon State Library

A view similar to the above photo, but several years later, circa 1940. *Published with permission of The Oregon State Library*

EDUCATION

The Methodist missionaries who helped settle the Willamette Valley had little success in their efforts to convert local American Indians to Christianity.

But along with their missionary fervor came a commitment to education, and the mid-valley remains home to two of the oldest institutions of learning in the West.

Willamette University grew out of missionary schools established in the 1840s. Chartered in 1853, it is one of the area's bedrock institutions – and the oldest college west of the Rockies.

The Chemawa Indian School has a similar distinction. Opened in Forest Grove in 1880 and moved to Salem five years later, it's the oldest continuously operated American Indian boarding school in the nation.

Salem's role as the state capital also has shaped education here. The state schools for the blind and deaf, established in the late 1800s, still operate today.

Throughout the area, some school buildings, having outlived their usefulness as places of learning, have found new lives. Downtown Salem's Garfield School survives as an office building. In Keizer, volunteers with visions of a community center are revamping the city's only historically significant public building: Keizer Elementary School, built in 1916.

Early staff of the *Clarion,* Salem High School's student newspaper. *Published with permission of The Oregon State Library*

Richmond School in Salem, circa 1913. The school opened in 1912.

The Washington Irving School, Silverton's first high school, was built in 1907. *Photo courtesy Silverton Country Historical Society*

Eola Elementary School, Polk County. This school opened in 1861.

Photo courtesy Al Jones

The Ralph Waldo Emerson School, Silverton, built in 1890. The school burned down during Christmas break, 1924. *Photo courtesy Silverton Country Historical Society*

North Salem School as it appeared in 1900. Built at a cost of $13,278.59 in 1890 at Market and Cottage streets, it was later remodeled and renamed Grant School. The building was razed in 1954 and replaced with Grant Grade School. *Published with permission of The Oregon State Library (B-6-4-A)*

Keizer School in 1916. This school was replaced by Cummings School in 1953. Cummings joined the Salem School District in 1955.

Sacred Heart Academy in Salem, circa 1889.

Published with permission of The Oregon State Library (B-6-8-B)

An artists drawing of the Sacred Heart Academy in Salem. The school was built in 1872 and razed in 1971.

Students in front of East School in Salem, circa 1900.
Published with permission of The Oregon State Library (B-6-14-B)

Washington School in Salem with its ornate west facade. The school was completed in 1887 at 12th and Center streets. It was known as East School until 1915 when the name was changed to Washington. The school was razed in 1949. *Published with permission of The Oregon State Library*

Students in front of Salem's Washington Elementary School in the mid-1940s. *Photo Courtesy Al Jones*

State School for the Deaf when it was located south of Salem. This building was built in 1895 and used until 1910. *Photo Courtesy Al Jones*

Oregon School for the Deaf in Salem was established in 1870 as the School for Deaf Mutes. It was relocated from Turner Road to the Locust Street campus in 1910 and renamed in 1913. Pictured is the class of 1906.

Oregon State School for the Deaf in North Salem. *Photo Courtesy Al Jones*

Oregon School for the Blind in Salem was established in 1870. Students are pictured in a typing class, circa 1921.

Park School, built in 1891 at 13th and Mission streets SE in Salem. The school was also known as Yew Park School.

Published with permission of The Oregon State Library (B-8-22-A)

Salem High School at Church and Marion streets opened in 1906.

Photo Courtesy Al Jones

Salem High School under construction in 1935-36. Parrish Junior High is visible in the top right corner. *Photo courtesy Connell Ward*

East Salem School. Mrs. Emma Kramer, teacher.

Published with permission of The Oregon State Library (B-6-12-13)

A class from Fern Ridge School, district 12, east of Salem, spring term.

Published with permission of The Oregon State Library (60-179)

Valsetz School prior to 1925.

A class at Lincoln Elementary School on High Street in Salem, 1895. Principal was Leon Graham Johnson. The teacher is thought to be Mrs. Nichols.

Published with permission of The Oregon State Library (B-6-5-B)

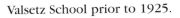

Victor Point School prior to 1915.

Sublimity Public School, 1887, E.A. Bennett teacher. Left to right, back row: Engel Schott, Perry Smith, August Klinger, Ed Gilbert, Tom Davey, Alvah Smith, Henry Smith, Bill Cooper, Bert Veal, Will Ledgerwood. Second row, left to right: Ethel Stanton, Olga Hobson, Jessie Hobson, Rhoda Hobson, Belle Stanton, Mamie Legerwood, Mr. Bennett, Ella Glover, Fannie Lee, Emma Udell, Nellie Lee, Hattie Clark, Celine Klinger, Lena Lee, Emma Miller, Otilla Becker. Front row; Left to right; Roy Miller, Alfred Klinger, Jim Udell, Art Gilbert, George Glover, Frank Hobson, George Pritchet, Dan Stanton, Price, unidentified, Joe Becker, Nona Lee, Amanda Becker. *Published with permission of The Oregon State Library (60-226)*

Sewing class at the Chemawa Indian School.

Published with permission of The Oregon State Library (B-7-7-A)

Chemawa Indian School campus. The school moved to Salem in 1885 from Forest Grove, where it opened in 1880. *Published with permission of The Oregon State Library (B-6-32-A)*

Chemawa Indian School, class of 1908. *Published with permission of The Oregon State Library*

An unidentified group of Chemawa Indian School students.

Published with permission of The Oregon State Library (B-6-22-A)

J. L. Parrish Junior High School, built in 1924.

Stayton 8th-grade graduating class, circa 1909.

Photo courtesy Santiam Historical Society

Sublimity College, circa 1883. The college was formally opened in 1858 after being granted a charter by the Legislative Assembly in Salem. The basic tuition rate in 1858 was $5 for the first 12-week term. The first teacher and president of the college was Milton Wright, who later became Bishop of the United Brethren Church. He also was the father of Orville and Wilbur Wright who became world famous pioneers of flight.

Photo courtesy Santiam Historical Society

Stayton High School 9th and 10th grade, circa 1912. Left to right, back row; Norman Davie, Steve Taylor, Arnold Funk, Everet Crabtree, George Tate. Middle row; Winnie Taylor, Malana Sustak, Bessie Clow, June Kearns, Pearl Doak, Roxie Staglon, Floyd Crabtree. Front row; Ed Blakely, Clarence Phillips, Paul Blakely.

Photo courtesy Santiam Historical Society.

The State Normal School main building(Campbell Hall) in Monmouth, 1905.
Photo courtesy Western Oregon University Archives

Oregon State Normal School faculty, 1905. The school has under-
gone seven name changes since its inception in 1857. It has also
been known as Oregon State School of Education, Western Oregon
State College and most recently, Western Oregon University. *Photo
courtesy Western Oregon University Archives*

Oregon State Normal School Class of 1897. *Photo courtesy Western Oregon University Archives*

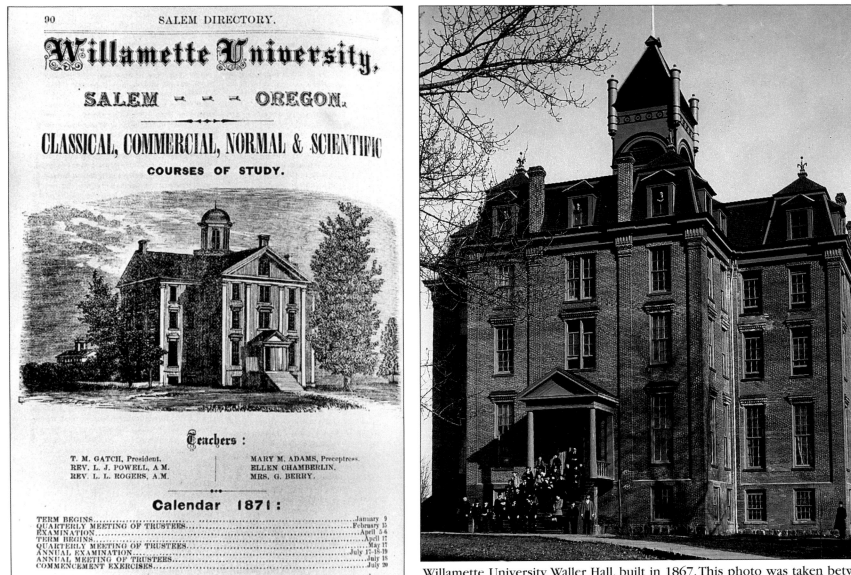

90　　　　SALEM DIRECTORY.

Willamette University,

SALEM – – – OREGON.

CLASSICAL, COMMERCIAL, NORMAL & SCIENTIFIC

COURSES OF STUDY.

Teachers :

T. M. GATCH, President.	MARY M. ADAMS, Preceptress.
REV. L. J. POWELL, A.M.	ELLEN CHAMBERLIN.
REV. L. L. ROGERS, A.M.	MRS. G. BERRY.

Calendar 1871 :

TERM BEGINS	January 9
QUARTERLY MEETING OF TRUSTEES	February 15
EXAMINATION	April 5-6
TERM BEGINS	April 17
QUARTERLY MEETING OF TRUSTEES	May 17
ANNUAL EXAMINATION	July 17-18-19
ANNUAL MEETING OF TRUSTEES	July 18
COMMENCEMENT EXERCISES	July 20

Willamette University directory from 1871.

Willamette University, Waller Hall, built in 1867. This photo was taken between 1891 and 1919. *Published with permission of The Oregon State Library (B-8-23-A)*

Willamette University's Eaton Hall, built 1907-1908.

Published with permission of The Oregon State Library

Willamette University College of Music on Winter Street SE. The building was also known as the Young Ladies' Hall. It is now the site of the brick Lausanne Hall which opened in 1920. *Published with permission of The Oregon State Library*

TRANSPORTATION

Since well before European settlers arrived, this part of the Willamette Valley has been vital to the business of coming and going.

Native trade routes between the coast and Oregon's interior passed through the same break in the Salem hills that provides passage for the north-flowing Willamette River.

The river eventually became an artery for lumber, logs and produce, and river transportation had much to do with the valley's early success.

Steamboats with names like Ruth, Ramona and Gypsy tied up at the foot of Salem's Trade Street in the late 1800s, and a sternwheeler, the City of Salem, offered river excursions from 1875 to 1895.

A growing Salem became a hub for roads and rails connecting smaller towns. And it developed its own forms of transport.

Horse-drawn streetcars showed up in 1889, only to be replaced that same year with an electric system.

By the 1890s, work was proceeding on the paving of muddy streets and the laying of concrete sidewalks.

The advent of the automobile brought still more change, from expansive car dealerships to the unrolling of Interstate 5. It also posed challenges that the Willamette Valley's pioneers could never imagine: traffic jams, parking crises and worries about smog.

A streetcar, April 4, 1904, at 7:00 a.m. at the west side of Commercial Street near Ferry Street. H.H. Churchill built the first three streetcars in Salem. *Published with permission of The Oregon State Library (B-12-2-A)*

City Express horse and wagon in Salem. *Published with permission of The Oregon State Library (B-13-2-A)*

Clifford and Maude Stayton with Tidal Wave on a Stayton street in the late 1800s. *Photo courtesy Santiam Historical Society*

This Dodge was driven up the Capitol steps to demonstrate the power of the new model, circa 1915.

Published with permission of The Oregon State Library

In 1903, George Graves, a pioneer motoring enthusiast in Salem, bought this red Rambler from Fred Wiggins, the town's first auto dealer. Fred received $900. During summer months, Graves used his Rambler extensively in his business; in winter it was stored. The motor was beneath the driver's seat and cranked from the side of the machine.

Automobile in front of the Dwight Misner Dodge dealership at Front and State streets in Salem, circa 1915.   *Published with permission of The Oregon State Library (B-22-2-C)*

This Southern Pacific Railroad underpass on the Pacific Highway North was completed in 1936. To the right is the Valley Packing Co. which produced Cascade meat products. *Published with permission of The Oregon State Library (WPA-4#1036)*

Roy E. King of Sublimity out for a drive in his car, circa 1916.

Photo courtesy Santiam Historical Society

Horse-drawn streetcars were used only in 1889. They were replaced by an electric system later that year. *Photo Courtesy Al Jones*

Salem streetcars, circa 1889.

Oregon Electric Railway, the "Champoeg."

Published with permission of The Oregon State Library

An Oregon Electric car at State and High streets in Salem, ready to leave for Portland in 1907. There is a parade in progress in the background.

Published with permission of The Oregon State Library (16-22)

Oregon Electric Railway, the "Sacajawea."

Published with permission of The Oregon State Library (10-37-A)

A southbound Oregon Electric Railway train stopped on High Street between State and Court streets in Salem, circa 1930.

Train pulling into Brooks Depot in the late 1930s. *Photo Courtesy Al Jones*

The second of three Southern Pacific stations in Salem as it appeared in 1913. *Published with permission of The Oregon State Library*

The Salem Oregon Electric Railroad on Front Street, circa 1913.

Published with permission of The Oregon State Library (19-7)

Engine No. 2 of the Willamina and Grand Ronde Railroad at Grand Ronde, circa 1900.

The first stage between Salem and Mill City operated in the early 1900s.
Photo courtesy Santiam Historical Society

A new bridge was built across the Santiam River after the old one washed out in 1909. *Photo courtesy Santiam Historical Society*

Bridge construction across the Santiam River in 1909. Note the work train on the bridge. *Published with permission of The Oregon State Library (10-12)*

Silverton Train Depot in 1913. *Photo courtesy Silverton Country Historical Society.*

Steamboats Ramona, Gypsy and Ruth at the foot of Trade Street in Salem during the flood of 1890. *Published with permission of The Oregon State Library (18-3)*

The sternwheeler "City of Salem" offered river excursions from 1875 to 1895. The Masonic Band entertained citizens on the Trade Street dock from the upper level of the boat in 1885. *Published with permission of The Oregon State Library*

Dr. H.H. Scovell (above on right, in front of plane), a local mechano-therapeutist, and Ben Taylor (above to the left of Scovell), a Salem postman, built this airplane in 1910. It was taken to the fairgrounds for testing and with Scovell (right) at the controls, barely cleared the ground. After three unsuccessful attempts at flight and three crashes, it was retired to become a State Fair exhibit.

Photos Courtesy Al Jones

COMMERCE

The Willamette Valley economy grew from some basics: agricultural richness and the availability of the Willamette River for transport.

Canneries, sawmills, fruit packing plants, processors of grain, flax and wool – all have seen economic prominence throughout the valley.

Factories sprang up along the riverfront in the 19th century, receiving raw materials and shipping away finished products on the Willamette.

From the day in 1848 that Thomas Cox of Illinois opened Salem's first store with merchandise he'd brought west by wagon, that city's downtown has been the area's economic hub.

Some downtown commercial buildings have enjoyed long histories.

The ornate Ladd and Bush bank, founded by Salem businessman Asahel Bush II, opened at State and Commercial streets in 1869.

The 11-story office tower at State and Liberty, now called Capitol Center, dates from 1927.

As the valley grew, other enterprises joined agriculture and timber as keys to the economy – state government, trade, manufacturing, services.

Now, the experts say, the economy of the Willamette Valley is among the most diversified in the nation.

Pacific Transfer and Auto Service Co. and Webb's Feed Barn at 216 Oak Street in Silverton. Photo taken May 12, 1921. *Photo courtesy Silverton Country Historical Society*

Exterior of Patton Bros. Books at 98 State Street in Salem.

Published with permission of The Oregon State Library (B-23-4-A)

Conrad Neibert's pool and card room in Stayton was an active place in 1908. Conrad tended bar. Customers are John Lau, Bill Cornish, Ernest Mathews, Evert Hobson, Marble Crabtree and Windle Freres.

Photo courtesy Santiam Historical Society

Interior of a drug store in downtown Salem.

Published with permission of The Oregon State Library (B-23-6-A)

Lewis Johnson Drug Store on Main Street in Silverton.
Photo courtesy Silverton Country Historical Society

The Confectionery in Sublimity, 1934. Ben Toepfer, proprietor, is behind the counter. *Photo courtesy Santiam Historical Society*

A Salem grocery store, circa 1900. *Photo courtesy Al Jones*

The interior of Steusloff Bros. Meat Market, located at the corner of Court and Liberty streets in Salem. *Published with permission of The Oregon State Library*

A Salem music store in the early 1900s.

Published with permission of The Oregon State Library (B-23-6-A)

Hattie Ficklin Paris, Stayton's first telephone switchboard operator.

Photo courtesy Santiam Historical Society

Operators from a Salem phone company pose for this photo in the early 1900s. *Published with permission of The Oregon State Library*

August Huckestein produced La Crona cigars in this typical cigar-making factory in Salem. Huckestein served as Salem postmaster in 1913.

Published with permission of The Oregon State Library

The Senator Hotel building, High at Court Street in Salem. *Photo courtesy Al Jones*

Interior of Silverton's Coolidge and McClaine Bank in the early 1900s. Pictured are Ed Adams, Alpha Smith and Martin Adams. *Photo courtesy Silverton Country Historical Society*

Reed Opera House building in Salem. The opera house operated from 1870 through 1900. *Photo courtesy Al Jones*

Grand Theatre at High and Court streets in Salem, built in 1900 by Odd Fellows Lodge. *Photo courtesy Al Jones*

The interior of the H.G. Meyer & Co. Barber Shop in Salem owned by H. George Meyer. *Published with permission of The Oregon State Library* (*B-23-20-A*)

Meeting of the Oregon Development League at the Marion Hotel on November 30, 1910. The building was built in 1870 as the Chemeketa House, became the Willamette Hotel in 1890 and finally the Marion Hotel in 1910. *Photo courtesy Al Jones*

Main Street in Silverton looking south toward Water Street with the covered bridge crossing Silver Creek in the distance.

Photo courtesy Silverton Country Historical Society

This 1880s view along the west side of Commercial Street at Ferry Street in Salem was taken from a window in the Chemeketa House. The building to the left is the Holman Building. *Published with permission of The Oregon State Library*

Automobiles in front of Steinbock Bros. Junk Co. in Salem.

Published with permission of The Oregon State Library (B-22-5-C)

State Street in Salem between Church and High streets, circa 1949. Photographed by Ben Maxwell. *Published with permission of The Oregon State Library*

Court Street in Salem between Church and High streets, circa 1949. Photographed by Ben Maxwell. *Published with permission of The Oregon State Library*

Court Street looking east from Front Street in Salem, circa 1949. Photographed by Ben Maxwell. *Published with permission of The Oregon State Library*

Commercial Street looking north toward State Street in Salem, circa 1949. Photographed by Ben Maxwell. *Published with permission of The Oregon State Library*

Employees in front of the Silverton Steam Laundry office in the late 1800s.
Photo courtesy Silverton Country Historical Society

William M. Hamilton, the first president of the Chamber of Commerce in Salem.

Stayton Steam Laundry on 1st Street. Pictured from left are Martha (Mattie) Dunagan, Stella Dunagan, Maude Dunagan, unidentified, Ezekial Dunagan, and unidentified.
Photo courtesy Santiam Historical Society

Masonic Lodge building on the corner of State and High streets in Salem. *Published with permission of The Oregon State Library (B-8-8-A)*

F.W. Pettyjohn Chevrolet on South Water Street, Silverton circa 1925. In 1926 it became Earl Hartman Chevrolet and in 1987, Bethany Automotive.

Photo courtesy Silverton Country Historical Society.

Mt. Angel Electric Line Depot, May, 1912.

Photo courtesy Silverton Country Historical Society

The J.C. Penney store at 160 North Liberty Street in Salem, circa 1930.

Published with permission of The Oregon State Library

Buren and Hamilton furniture store in Salem on Commercial Street, 1895.
Published with permission of The Oregon State Library

In 1892 this building was the site of the first basketball game played in the Northwest. The building was located in Salem on the northwest corner of Chemeketa and Commercial streets and was used by the YMCA and Willamette University. *Published with permission of The Oregon State Library*

Chicago Store in Salem before the roads were paved. *Photo courtesy Al Jones*

State Street at Commercial Street in Salem looking east, circa 1900. An oculist had hung "spectacles" over the street. *Photo courtesy Al Jones*

Cook's Hotel at the southeast corner of High and State street in Salem. The hotel was built in 1864 by Joseph Miller and razed in 1926. It was also known as Monroe House and Cherry City Hotel.

Attorney Van Valkenberg in his office in Silverton. Photo taken May 30, 1912. *Photo courtesy Silverton Country Historical Society*

Weller Bros. Groceries and Provisions used this wagon and horses to make deliveries in Salem. *Published with permission of The Oregon State Library (B-13-4-A)*

Commercial Street from State Street in Salem, looking toward the Marion Hotel, circa 1880. *Photo courtesy Al Jones*

Third Street in Stayton, looking south, circa 1945.

Photo courtesy Santiam Historical Society

Main Street in Dallas, circa 1874.

Sung Lung's Chinese laundry in 1889, Court Street, Salem. *Photo courtesy Al Jones*

Salem Brewery Association building, built in the late 1880s at the northeast corner of Commercial and Trade streets. It became Sick's Brewery in 1943, named for Emil Sick. Its major brand was Sick's Select. The building was razed in 1955. *Photo courtesy Al Jones*

The White House Restaurant at 362 State Street in Salem. *Photo courtesy Al Jones*

The Bligh building on State Street between High and Liberty in Salem. The Bligh Theatre operated from 1911 to 1927. *Photo courtesy Al Jones*

Timber workers employed by Cobbs and Mitchell Co. at Camp Six near Valsetz in 1928.

Silver Falls Timber Co. outside of Silverton, circa 1920s. *Photo courtesy Silverton Country Historical Society*

Stoltz cider and vinegar plant on South Summer Street between Mill and Bellevue streets in Salem. *Published with permission of The Oregon State Library (B-21-5-A)*

Early industrial shop in Salem.

Published with permission of The Oregon State Library (B-29-13-A)

Freres Lumber Co.'s first log truck, circa 1930.

Photo courtesy Santiam Historical Society

This mill was built in 1875 in Parkersville. Also pictured is a grain wagon, two buggies, men and boys, circa 1890. *Published with permission of The Oregon State Library*

Silverton Lumber Co.'s logging train. *Photo courtesy Silverton Country Historical Society*

Silver Falls Logging Co. worker with a train-load of logs.

Photo courtesy Silverton Country Historical Society

This mill in the town of Black Rock in Polk County provided the community's only income. Black Rock was the western terminus of the Southern Pacific Co. branch line west from Dallas. The logs were transported by train. The rails were removed after World War II. *Published with permission of The Oregon State Library*

Fischer's Flouring Mill on South Water Street in Silverton. The small building in the middle is now Fischer's Community Center.
Photo courtesy Silverton Country Historical Society

Ethelbert C. Case traveled for Dr. Baker's Medicines, Extracts and Spices in Salem and its countryside, circa 1915. *Published with permission of The Oregon State Library (B-13-1-A)*

The Capital Lumbering Co. at the foot of Ferry Street was the principal sawmill in the Salem vicinity from 1866 to 1914. Photo circa 1901.
Published with permission of The Oregon State Library (B-21-2-A)

AGRICULTURE

Agricultural products and practices have come and gone.

No longer is the valley known as a center for the growing and processing of flax. No longer is peppermint harvested with hand scythes.

But this reality remains: Agriculture has shaped Willamette Valley communities from the beginning, infused their culture, propelled their economies.

During the great westward migrations of the last century, those with visions of gold headed for California. But those inclined toward farming steered their wagons to Oregon. The Eden at the end of the Oregon Trail was the Willamette Valley.

Generations of children have worked summers picking beans, strawberries or other produce, although the tradition now has faded, largely because of child labor laws.

Generations of college students have toiled summers in canneries, and some still do.

Salem long has been known as the Cherry City, and for a time earlier this century, the now-gone Cherry Fair passed up Independence Day as Salem's major municipal event. Other communities, too, have festivals honoring their agricultural products.

Agriculture remains vital to the local economy. Marion County produces more than $400 million of agricultural products a year, ranking it first among Oregon's 36 counties.

Hop harvest in 1910 on the Alvis Brunner farm in the Evergreen area.

Photo courtesy Silverton Country Historical Society

Men harvesting flax. *Published with permission of The Oregon State Library (WPA-4#589)*

Wigrich Ranch hop harvest take-off crew in 1930, south of Independence.

Photo courtesy Al Jones

View of the rural area near the Oregon School for the Deaf in Salem. Students worked in the field hoeing and plowing. Two teams of farm horses are also shown with a large garden area in the foreground and farm buildings in the back. Photo circa 1916.

Threshing team and equipment in 1891. P. Hiebert owned the equipment. *Published with permission of The Oregon State Library (B-43-53-A)*

Threshing equipment and unidentified crew on a farm in the Willamette Valley. *Published with permission of The Oregon State Library (N-43-8-A)*

Threshing crew on the Spenner farm east of Sublimity.

Photo courtesy Santiam Historical Society

Haying on a Willamette Valley farm. Several women, dressed in fancy clothes, watch.

Truck and wagon loaded with flax. Plant storage shed is in the background. *Published with permission of The Oregon State Library (WPA-4#599)*

Flax scutching plant. *Published with permission of The Oregon State Library (WPA-4 #457)*

Interior of a flax storage shed. *Published with permission of The Oregon State Library (WPA-4 #473)*

WPA offices and flax weighing shed.
Published with permission of The Oregon State Library (WPA-4 #596)

Processing tanks for flax. *Published with permission of The Oregon State Library (WPA-4 #598)*

Lake Labish celery harvest. *Published with permission of The Oregon State Library (WPA-4 #2023)*

Hop harvesting. *Published with permission of The Oregon State Library (WPA-4 #551)*

A Willamette Valley hop kiln in 1936. *Photo courtesy Al Jones*

A load of hops on its way to storage, circa 1930. *Photo courtesy Al Jones*

Ripe Italian prunes were shaken from the trees and picked up from the ground. This photo was taken in the Dallas area.

Published with permission of The Oregon State Library (WPA-4 #870)

Harvesting peppermint with hand scythes near Salem.

Published with permission of The Oregon State Library (WPA-4 #563)

Early mule powered combine tractor.

Published with permission of The Oregon State Library (29-2)

Cone's hop yard. John Rabens (sitting) with hounds; Henry Benson, standing behind John, circa 1895. *Published with permission of The Oregon State Library (60-170A)*

Women packing dehydrated loganberries in a Salem packing plant, circa 1905.

Published with permission of The Oregon State Library

RURAL LIFE

They worked in the woods, cutting giant firs with the two-handled saws known as misery whips. They pushed roads and railroads up the river canyons of the Cascade and Coast ranges. Or they homesteaded in remote places, hauling their produce to market in horse-drawn wagons on rutted roads.

They were the folk who populated the villages and towns that dot the rural areas of the Willamette Valley landscape.

Many of them gave their names to the places where they lived, a legacy that remains today. Zena in Polk County is named for Arvazena Cooper, who moved to the place with her husband in 1863. The Gates family gave its name to a hamlet in the North Santiam Canyon.

Some place names hint at the origins of the people who came west to inhabit these small towns.

Detroit, not far from Gates, was so named because it was home to a number of immigrants from Michigan.

Rural life can be tenuous, and some places have vanished from the map. Valsetz, a Polk County sawmill town built in 1918, faded away in 1984. By then, it was more practical to haul logs to modern mills in bigger cities.

The Gates family. Gates, Oregon was named for Mary Ann Gates. Standing, left to right: Gertrude, Belle and Lizzie. Seated are Albert and Mary Ann Gates, and son, Bert. The town was originally Gatesville.
Published with permission of The Oregon State Library (60-65)

William Andrew Rains and his bride, May McMillen-Rains, of Salem. Andrew, called "Ammie," was reared near Mill City. The marriage took place August 26, 1893, in Salem. *Published with permission of The Oregon State Library (60-29b)*

Road work crew near Mill City. Left to right: George Gist, Elvie Taylor, Al Mulkey, F. Snyder, Oscar Doke, Marion Taylor, Charlie Work, Road Supervisor, and F. Snyder. *Published with permission of The Oregon State Library (60-67)*

Andrew R. Siegmund, hauling wheat to market east of Salem. His horses' names were Prince and Tom. *Published with permission of The Oregon State Library (60-74)*

Mehama looking west along what is now Highway 22. The large building at the left is the hotel owned and operated by James X. Smith and his wife, Mehama, for whom the town was named.

Published with permission of The Oregon State Library (60-42)

Public auction of cows on Sublimity Public School grounds. Photo was taken in the early 1930s. The site is now City Hall and the Early Pioneers Park.

Photo courtesy Santiam Historical Society

An early view of Mill City.

Street scene in St. Paul.

Published with permission of The Oregon State Library WPA-4#125

Photo taken in Coon Hollow. Among those pictured are: Julia Siegmund, Henry Benson, Etta Cornish, Wesley Riggs, Minnie Ireton, Alice Cornish and Louis Siegmund.

Published with permission of The Oregon State Library (60-238)

Earl and Ethel Cross with their pet dog and fawn.

Published with permission of The Oregon State Library (60-234)

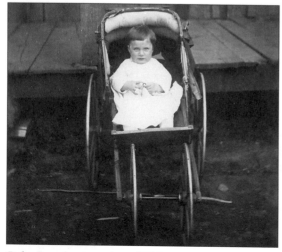

Baby in a buggy, circa 1900.

Published with permission of The Oregon State Library (60-98)

Reunion of pioneers in 1874 at the Aurora Grove. *Published with permission of The Oregon State Library (WPA-4 #985)*

This church in St. Paul is said to be the oldest brick Catholic church west of the Rocky Mountains.

Main Street in Independence, 1910.

The Turner Memorial Tabernacle, built in 1891.

The community of Shaw, east of Salem, circa 1905

A view of Dallas with the Polk County Courthouse on the right.

A gas station in Brooks in the early 1940's. *Photo courtesy Al Jones*

Ryan's Store in Butteville. *Published with permission of The Oregon State Library (WPA-4 #121)*

Wild blackberry pickers. Standing, left to right: Elvie Taylor, Mrs. Marion Taylor, Marion Taylor, Mae Taylor and Mary Fisher. Sitting, left to right: Louis Fisher, and Andrew Fisher. *Published with permission of The Oregon State Library (60-64)*

Benjamin Hayden, grandfather of Ben Maxwell, circa1890. He came to Polk County in 1852 and became judge in the 1860s. In 1870, he was the Polk County representative and later became speaker of the Oregon House of Representatives.

The Davenport family, Silverton. Famous cartoonist Homer Davenport is standing. *Photo courtesy Al Jones*

Jim Hogan in the center, Jim Collins on the left, and Bill Des, on the right, in Gates. *Published with permission of The Oregon State Library (60-87)*

Aurora Colony band. A.H. Giesy, Emanuel Kiel, Fred Giesy, Henry Giesy, William Giesy, and Fred Will Sr.

A hunting party on the North Santiam. The first man to the left is Louis Blakely. The woman in the chair with a book is Lizzie Huber.

Steamers "Ruth" and "Oregona" at the Champoeg landing, 1907.

The first meeting of the Oregon Pioneer Association held at Champoeg May 2, 1901. The group is unveiling a monument commemorating the 1843 vote to create the Oregon Territory. The monument names the signers of the petition.

RESIDENTIAL

Some are humble, some ornate and stately. Many are somewhere in the middle. Taken together, homes define neighborhoods, give clues about those who first lived in them, and link past with present.

Asahel Bush II, founder of the Oregon Statesman newspaper and the Ladd and Bush Bank, built what may be Salem's best-known house. Finished in 1878, the Bush House is a simplified Victorian at the fringe of what is now Bush's Pasture Park. Open to the public, it is part of the area's public heritage.

One of Salem's greatest assets is the opportunity to live close to downtown, in historic neighborhoods once occupied by prosperous farmers, high government officials and businessmen.

Not all historic houses, however, have survived.

A colonial house on Cottage Street NE, once home to George F. Rodgers, mayor from 1907 to 1910, was cleared away in 1997 to make room for a parking lot.

Throughout the valley, houses large and small attest to our pioneer past – such as a log house near Aurora, and a farmhouse near Champoeg that has been in the same family for 130 years.

John Gulliver West drives the carriage while his daughter, Nean West sits sidesaddle; his son Fred West holds a horse, and his grandson Walter West sits on the steps of the West home at Oak and University streets, Salem, in 1895. Oswald West, John's son and future governor, was not present for this photo.
Published with permission of The Oregon State Library (B-16-2-A)

The Zorn homestead house, water tower and barn near Champoeg, built 1867-70. The house is still in the Zorn family.

Published with permission of The Oregon State Library

The John Stauffer Sr. log house south of Aurora, built in 1869.

The Bush house, built by Asahel Bush II in 1877-1878. *Photo courtesy Al Jones*

Deepwood House, built in 1894 by Dr. Luke A. Port.

Published with permission of The Oregon State Library (B-38-22-A)

Thomas Brunk House, west of Salem in Polk County, 1860.

Published with permission of The Oregon State Library (WPA-4 #870)

Jacob Conser House, the old Hotel Jefferson, built in 1854.

Published with permission of The Oregon State Library (WPA-4 #113)

The Julius Alm family home in Silverton, built by Alm in 1895. Photo taken in 1917 by J.D. Drake. *Photo courtesy Silverton Country Historical Society*

President Herbert Hoover's boyhood home, located at 2213 Hazel Avenue, in Northeast Salem. *Photo courtesy Al Jones*

An old colony house, located one mile northwest of Aurora. This house was built in the 1860s. *Published with permission of The Oregon State Library (WPA-4#643)*

A sketch of the old Mission House (Jason Lee Mission House), built in 1834-1835 north of today's Salem.

Published with permission of The Oregon State Library (WPA-4 #387)

The Holman residence, 1887. *Photo courtesy Al Jones*

Residence of E.N. Cooke, Court Street, 1887, later the home of the Patton family. *Photo courtesy Al Jones*

The Settlemier House in Woodburn, built in 1889 by Jesse Settlemier, founder of Woodburn. *Photo by Richard Stefani, courtesy Smith Western, Inc.*

This home, built in Dallas in 1892, was moved to Pedee in 1979.

Postman Ben Taylor riding his bicycle in front of the Eugene Breyman home in 1887. *Photo courtesy Al Jones*

Sam Brown House on Pacific Highway, built in 1856-1858 near Gervais. *Published with permission of The Oregon State Library (WPA-4 #113)*

PUBLIC SERVICE

It took 15 years of arguments, elections and competition among towns that wanted the honor. But in 1864, Salem became Oregon's permanent state capital. It was the city's defining event.

The Capitol, topped by a gleaming golden pioneer statue, dominates the skyline – and anchors a broad swath of imposing state office buildings, including the state library and the elegant home of the Supreme Court.

State government is a presence in other parts of the area, too, from the Oregon State Hospital to the state penitentiary and specialized schools for the blind and deaf.

State employees – bureaucrats, laborers, corrections officers, computer experts and more – form a substantial portion of the work force.

The Legislature convenes for six months every other year, drawing lawmakers, lobbyists and hangers-on from all corners of Oregon, and boosting the local economy.

Oregonians are as proficient as anyone when it comes to complaining about the cost of government.

But economists say state government has been good for the local economy, helping to smooth out the highs and lows of other business sectors.

The Capitol in 1888 after the columns and porticoes were added. The dome was added in 1893.

Published with permission of The Oregon State Library (B-4-2-B)

The Capitol, looking east from Cottage Street, beyond the Breyman Brothers Fountain erected in 1903-1904. The "Pioneer" on top fell off the memorial about 1916. *Published with permission of The Oregon State Library* (B-4-3)

The Capitol before the April 25, 1935 fire. The Circuit Rider statue remains on the grounds today. The statue was dedicated in 1924.

Photo courtesy Al Jones

The Capitol, after the E.M. Waite Memorial Fountain was installed in 1912.

The Capitol, circa 1900. *Published with permission of The Oregon State Library (2-34-B)*

Salem City Hall. *Published with permission of The Oregon State Library*

This drawing of Oregon's first Capitol in 1854 was done by Murray Wade from descriptions he acquired from the Library of Congress. Wade never actually saw the building, which burned in 1855. *Photo courtesy Al Jones*

Salem Public Library at State and Winter streets. Construction of the building was funded by the Andrew Carnegie Foundation and was completed in 1912.
Published with permission of The Oregon State Library

City workers on State Street near 12th Street, 1907. *Published with permission of The Oregon State Library (B-4-2-B)*

Marion County Courthouse in Salem, prior to 1905. The courthouse was built in 1872 and razed in 1952.

Published with permission of The Oregon State Library (B-8-3-A)

The Polk County Courthouse at Court and Main streets in Dallas, circa 1900. The courthouse was completed in 1898 after the original county courthouse burned, along with much of Main Street, during the fire of 1897. The rock used in construction was quarried from a limestone pit between Dallas and Falls City.

The old Polk County Courthouse in Dallas. This picture was taken prior to 1897, when the building burned. Polk County was created by the provisional legislature on December 22, 1845. It was named for James Knox Polk, then president of the United States. Dallas was named for George Mifflin Dallas, vice president of the United States from 1845 to 1849.

Oregon State Hospital, (The Insane Asylum) Dome Building north of Center Street, Salem. . *Published with permission of The Oregon State Library*

Oregon State Hospital (the Insane Asylum), Salem. *Published with permission of The Oregon State Library*

The east end of the State Penitentiary in Salem. *Published with permission of The Oregon State Library*

Salem Post Office, many years prior to being moved in 1938.

Published with permission of The Oregon State Library

Fred Gunning, rural mail carrier from the Salem Post Office, circa 1907.

Salem Post Office and the Evening Capital Journal, Commercial Street south of Ferry Street on the west side.

Moving the old stone block post office, February 15, 1938. The building is now Willamette University's Gatke Hall at 12th and State streets.

These men were Salem mail carriers, and the post office was in the corner building later occupied by the Statesman Journal circulation department. Pictured are: John Farrar at the far left. He later became the Salem Postmaster from 1922-1934. The group also includes the city's first carrier, appointed July 1, 1887, George Hatch, (seated in front) an uncle of Farrar. At the back is Si Howard. In line with Farrar are Charles Cosper, Ben Taylor, the city's second carrier, and Amos Long. Farrar, who resided at 267 North Cottage Street, became a postman, November 23, 1899.

Oregon State Hospital grounds west of the institution, which had been moved from Portland in 1883. *Published with permission of The Oregon State Library*

Supreme Court building, 12th and State streets in Salem.

Published with permission of The Oregon State Library

Ed Hirsch, Salem postmaster, 1898-1906, after serving as state treasurer.

State Home for the Feeble Minded, Salem. *Photo courtesy Al Jones*

The 1927 Oregon Supreme Court. Pictured from left to right: Justices George M. Brown, Oliver P. Coshow, John L. Rand, Chief Justice George H. Burnett, Justices Thomas A. McBride, Harry H. Belt, and Henry J. Bean.

Published with permission of The Oregon State Library (29-64)

Stayton Fire Department Drill Team participating in a fireman's muster in Albany. *Photo courtesy Santiam Historical Society*

Salem Fire Department in the early years. *Photo courtesy Al Jones*

Salem policemen in 1885. From left: Linn Smith, unidentified, and Wells LaTourette. *Photo courtesy Al Jones*

The Salem Fire Department exhibits its steam pumpers on Court Street, circa 1906. *Photo courtesy Al Jones*

Early Salem Fire Department, in the old city hall at High and Chemeketa streets. All city firemen were volunteers until 1903, when the first paid firefighter was hired. *Photo courtesy Al Jones*

Silverton Fire Department in the 1920s.

Photo courtesy Silverton Country Historical Society

Yew Park hose team, circa 1895.

Published with permission of The Oregon State Library (B-46-1)

Salem Fire Department during a July 4th celebration in 1890.

Firemen in the early years. *Photo courtesy Al Jones*

Members of the Salem Police Department, year unknown. *Published with permission of The Oregon State Library*

DISASTERS

Disasters of many kinds mar Willamette Valley history.

Stunned crowds watched long into the night on April 25, 1935, when fire demolished the Capitol, itself the replacement of a Capitol that had burned in 1855.

Downtown Salem's venerable Marion Hotel burned in 1971.

Among natural disasters, the Columbus Day Storm of Oct. 12, 1962 was among the most fearsome. It came out of nowhere, with windspeeds in the Willamette Valley as high as 125 miles per hour, causing massive damage. Twenty-four people died across Oregon.

The Willamette River, a source of beauty and prosperity, often has turned nasty, unleashing vicious floods.

Among the worst years: 1861, 1890, 1964 and 1996.

During the 1964 flood, which struck just before Christmas, the National Guard evacuated almost 300 people from Salem Memorial Hospital. The February flood of 1996 brought more misery and more evacuations, particularly along Mill Creek.

In spite of this history, the valley's biggest calamity may have yet to strike. Scientists say much of western Oregon and Washington could be due for an enormous earthquake – although no one knows exactly when.

Train wreck on November 12, 1890, at Lake Labish in Keizer.
Published with permission of The Oregon State Library (10-39J)

Train wreck at Bridge No. 137 in Salem. *Published with permission of The Oregon State Library (10-40A)*

Train wreck on O.C. & E. Railroad at tunnel No. 1, April 29, late 1890s.

Published with permission of The Oregon State Library (10-1)

Train wreck at Lake Labish, Keizer, November 12, 1890.

Published with permission of The Oregon State Library (10-39I)

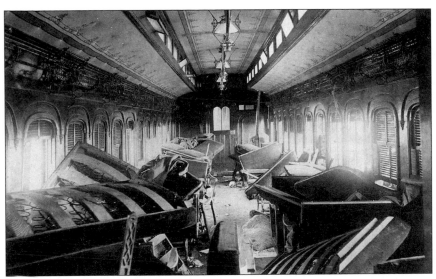

Interior of the train wreck at Lake Labish, Keizer. November 12, 1890.
Published with permission of The Oregon State Library (10-39D)

Train wreck at Lake Labish, Keizer. November 12, 1890.
Published with permission of The Oregon State Library (10-39E)

Train wreck at Lake Labish, Keizer. November 12, 1890.
Published with permission of The Oregon State Library (10-39A)

Train wreck at Lake Labish, Keizer. November 12, 1890.
Published with permission of The Oregon State Library (10-39F)

The engineer Jack Miller was killed in this train wreck. *Published with permission of The Oregon State Library (10-41)*

State Capitol burning on April 25, 1935.

Aerial view of the Capitol after the fire.

Published with permission of The Oregon State Library (2-28)

The bridge over the creek on South Commercial Street during the 1890 flood.
Photo courtesy Al Jones

The 1890 flood destroyed many homes, as well as the High Street bridge and covered bridge. *Photo courtesy Al Jones*

High Street bridge during the February 1890 flood. This view is looking north from Fry Hill. *Photo courtesy Al Jones*

The Salem flood of 1890, looking across the Willamette River to the east.

The 1935 Opera House fire in Silverton. *Photo courtesy Silverton Country Historical Society*

Looking down Oak Street to Water Street, the day after the Opera House fire in Silverton. *Photo courtesy Silverton Country Historical Society*

The sternwheeler "Relief" encased in ice when the Willamette River froze over at Salem in December of 1924.

An overhead view of the Guardian Building fire, November 3, 1947. *Photo courtesy Al Jones*

The Guardian Building fire of November 3, 1947. The building was located at 404 State Street on the corner of State and Liberty streets. This view is from street level on the west side. *Photo courtesy Al Jones*

MEDICAL

Salem Hospital was incorporated on New Year's Day in 1896 with $752 raised from churches and public-spirited citizens.

It was the beginning of a tradition of community-guided, not-for-profit hospital operation that continues to this day.

The early years were trying. The hospital borrowed various quarters, including McKinley School, until a permanent building could be finished on Center Street NE.

Another hospital arose from similarly humble roots. The Mennonite Sisters opened Deaconess Hospital with four nurses in 1916, in a building that a short time earlier had been a hotel.

Deaconess, which became Salem Memorial Hospital in 1947 when the Mennonites turned it over to the community, expanded many times.

Bricks were salvaged from a closed-down mill for one addition, and from an old Newberg hotel for another.

For decades, Salem had two hospitals: Salem Memorial, at Winter and Oak streets SE, and the old Salem Hospital, renamed Salem General, on Center Street. It was an arrangement that couldn't withstand the costs and complexities of modern medicine.

The hospitals merged in 1969 into a single, not-for-profit institution.

Salem General Hospital's first graduate nurses in 1889, including Grace Taylor (back row, left) who became Marion County's first public health nurse. *Photo courtesy Al Jones*

Oregon State Hospital, built in 1883. *Photo courtesy Al Jones*

Deaconess Hospital at Winter Street SE, which became Salem Memorial Hospital and later Salem Hospital. *Photo courtesy Al Jones*

Oregon State T.B. Hospital, east of Salem, now the site of Western Baptist Bible College.

The former Boys and Girls Aid Society's Glen Oak Orphanage, pictured in 1900 after it became Salem Hospital. After 1916 the structure housed the Oregon State Hospital nurses; then it was razed.

Published with permission of The Oregon State Library (B-8-29)

An early photo of a group of nurses, circa 1889.

Photo courtesy Al Jones

Salem Memorial Hospital started in this two-story frame building in 1916 as Deaconess Hospital.

Salem doctors in the 1870s. Standing in back, from left to right: Dr. Payton and Dr. Lingo. Front row, from left to right: Dr. Carpenter, Dr. Rice, Dr. Fisk and Dr. Boswell.

CELEBRATION & RECREATION

Fairs, parades, festivals, professional baseball games – the Willamette Valley has had them all, although some have come and gone from the landscape.

Baseball, in particular, has had a spotty history, one sketched by such teams as the Salem Senators, the Salem Dodgers and, in a gleaming new stadium opened in 1997, the Salem-Keizer Volcanoes.

Other celebrations have been more constant. After an inaugural year in Oregon City, the Oregon State Fair moved to Salem in 1862, and has remained ever since.

One celebration, the Cherry Fair, was intended to honor Salem's self-conferred distinction as the world's Cherry City. The festivities included a parade and the selection of a yearly King Bing.

Area residents have turned out over the years for many other diversions: Fourth of July parades downtown, summer concerts in Marion Square and Willson Park, the Salem Art Fair and Festival in Bush's Pasture Park, and Vaudeville shows at such theaters as the Elsinore, which opened in 1926.

Throughout the valley, communities have organized festivals to celebrate their bounty, honoring everything from strawberries and beans to corn and mushrooms.

All dressed up for the Salem Cherry Fair. Asahel Bush IV is in the rickshaw. This photo was taken at the basement door of the Willis Duniway home, 925 Court Street in Salem between 1908 and 1913.

Published with permission of The Oregon State Library (21-1)

Salem Cherry Festival parade, circa 1920s. *Published with permission of The Oregon State Library (B-10-9-A)*

Queen Agnes Gilbert, Salem's first Cherry Festival Queen, 1903.
Photo courtesy Al Jones

A young girl dressed up and ready for a Salem parade, circa 1910.

Published with permission of The Oregon State Library (B-10-8-A)

Cherry Festival Parade in 1913, looking west on State Street. *Photo courtesy Al Jones*

Salem Cherry Festival parade, 1916. The Cherrians are walking by the queen's chariot. *Photo courtesy Al Jones*

Fourth of July parade in downtown Stayton, circa 1909.
Photo courtesy Santiam Historical Society

An entry in a Silverton Fourth of July parade in the early 1900s. *Photo courtesy Silverton Country Historical Society*

Silverton Fourth of July parade, 1914. *Photo courtesy Silverton Country Historical Society*

Crowds fill Main Street in Silverton after the July 4th parade of 1912.
Photo courtesy Silverton Country Historical Society

State Fair in the mid 1940s. *Published with permission of The Oregon State Library (29-6)*

Stock parade at the State Fair, 1911.
Published with permission of The Oregon State Library (29-6)

State Fair in the mid 1940s. *Published with permission of The Oregon State Library (29-6)*

Fourth of July parade in Silverton, circa 1915.

Photo courtesy Silverton Country Historical Society

Detroit and the Santiam Canyon were a popular recreational area even in the 1940s, when this photo was taken. *Photo courtesy Santiam Historical Society*

Burning the "Kaiser" in Silverton, November 11, 1918.

Photo courtesy Silverton Country Historical Society

A parade in Independence near the turn of the century.

Political rally at the northwest corner of Chemeketa and Commercial streets in 1914. James Withycombe was elected governor in 1915. George Chamberlain ran successfully for his second term as U.S. Senator during the same year.

Published with permission of The Oregon State Library

A Stayton entry in the victory parade, November 11, 1918, in Salem.

Photo courtesy Santiam Historical Society

Crowds watched a spontaneous victory parade march west on Court Street on November 11, 1918. Salem men in the 3rd Infantry had gone to France in December 1917 and returned from World War I to great fanfare.

People jammed into downtown Salem for a Fourth of July parade in the late 1800s. *Published with permission of The Oregon State Library (B-10-4-A)*

Willamette University Band. Members included Walter Winslow, William Zimmerman, W.H. Winans, L.H. Graham, Austin C. Price, N.B. Moser, O.K. Wolfe, Harry Swafford, Glen Unruh, Roy Nutt, and Ivan Martin. *Published with permission of The Oregon State Library (B-27-3-A)*

115th Cavalry at the Marion Hotel, April 1942, during World War II. *Photo courtesy Al Jones*

Sacred Heart Academy women's musical string orchestra.
Published with permission of The Oregon State Library (B-27-1-A)

The Stayton Cornet Band, circa 1890. Back row, left to right: Fay Wrightman, Charley Brown, George Hollister, Frank Thomas, Frank Caspell, Louis Siegmund, Grant Lake and Joe Kearns. Front row, left to right: York Richardson, George Caspell, Ed Nixon, William Lake, Beecher Lake and Joe Lake.

Published with permission of The Oregon State Library (B-27-1-A)

Opening day ceremony at the Star Theater in Stayton, circa 1914. A small band and pianist, lower left, accompanied the screen images. The musicians each earned about $1 per evening. *Photo courtesy Santiam Historical Society*

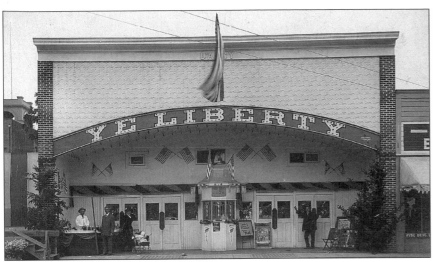

Liberty Theater at 170 North Commercial Street North, Salem.

Published with permission of The Oregon State Library (16-19)

The old Liberty Theater, east side of Liberty between State and Court streets, 1918. *Published with permission of The Oregon State Library*

State Theater on Church Street North.

Published with permission of The Oregon State Library

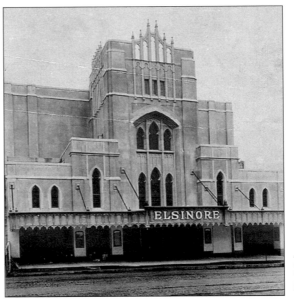

An early view of the Elsinore Theatre, built in 1926.

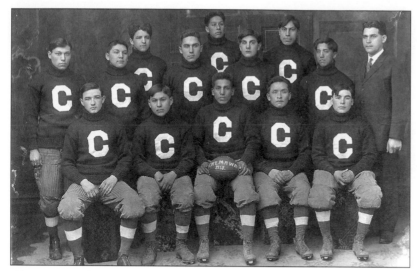

Chemawa Indian School boys football team, 1913.

Published with permission of The Oregon State Library (B-7-18-A)

Chemawa Indian School girl's basketball champions, 1913.

Published with permission of The Oregon State Library (B-26-3-A)

Oregon School for the Deaf baseball team.

Published with permission of The Oregon State Library (C-35-25)

The 1909 Silverton High School state championship basketball team.

Photo courtesy Silverton Country Historical Society

Salem baseball team, circa 1926.

Photo courtesy Al Jones

Willamette's Bearcat football team of 1906.

The Salem College (business college), baseball team of 1872. Front row: Prof. John Garrison, George Richards, James McDully, Bliss Rickey and Oscar Taylor. Back row: James Colemand, Preston Smith, George Belt and John Forsythe.

The 1945 Stayton High School basketball team. Left to right; Don Nielson, Ron Johnson, Bill Freele, Enoch Samples, Richard Duncan, Wayne Lierman, Albert Solberg and Marcel Van Driesche.
Photo courtesy Santiam Historical Society

The 1905 Willamette University girls basketball team, described in the yearbook as "…the pluckiest girls that ever bloomed forth in bloomers." *Photo courtesy Al Jones*

Marion County baseball champions, 1936. Pictured is, Glen Morioko, Ivan McCoy, Masao Tamiyasn, Les Lowery, Bus Cowe, Dick Gallagher, Ray Potts, Clifford Bishop, O.G. Lowery, Rob Bailey, Carl Steelhammer. *Photo courtesy Al Jones*

Salem High School, 1915 state champion basketball team. Roy S. "Spec" Keene (fourth from the left in the back row) later was a three sport star and coached in three sports for 17 seasons at Willamette University (1926-1942).

Photo courtesy Al Jones

The Oregon State Normal School indoor baseball championship team of 1904. *Photo courtesy Western Oregon University Archives*

The Salem Senators, 1941. Front row; left to right; Eddie Adams, catcher, Del Oliver, pitcher, Fred Lanifero, second base, Jack Warren, outfield/first base, Frank Dieriecx, pitcher, Bob Williams, catcher, Bunny Griffiths, manager/short-stop. Back row, left to right, Lee Fallin, pitcher, Charlie Petersen, outfield, Clint Cameron, outfield/first base, Bob Bergstrom, outfield, Al Lightner, third/first base, Chet Simpson, pitcher, Roy Helser, pitcher, Duke Windsor, pitcher. *Photo courtesy Al Jones*

George E. Waters, owner of the Salem Senators baseball team at the construction site of Waters Field, circa 1940. *Photo courtesy Al Jones*

"Biddie" Bishop's baseball grounds, near 12th and Yew Park streets, SE. This was the home of the semi-pro Salem Senators, circa 1920. *Photo courtesy Al Jones*

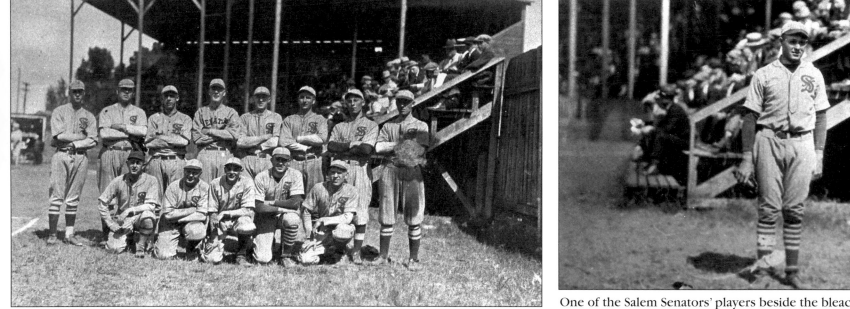

The Salem semi-pro team the Senators, 1924. *Photo courtesy Al Jones*

One of the Salem Senators' players beside the bleachers.

Photo courtesy Al Jones

Salem High School, 1920 champions. This is the team that edged out Lincoln High School of Portland 12-11 in the state basketball finals. Lincoln led 11-10 with 40 seconds remaining, but fouled (double dribbled), and A.T. "Slats" Gill missed the free throw. His brother, Luke, tipped the ball in for the winning basket. Pictured in the back row, left to right, rear: Earl Shafer, Luke Gill, Breyman Boise, Will Ashby, Amory T. "Slats" Gill and Jack Randal. Front; Guy Jones, Coach Jacob G. Schott and Paul Staley. "Slats" Gill was later the head coach at Oregon State University from 1928 to 1955. *Photo courtesy Al Jones*

A Stayton baseball team in 1911. Left to right; Billie Ortman, John Thomas, Jim Burton, Byron Robertson, Fitz Goodman, Herb Humphrey, Luther Cole, Havey Beauchamp and Frank Van Nyse. *Photo courtesy Santiam Historical Society*